Bipolar

The Mind

HATTIE LEWIS

PAGE PUBLISHING, INC.
New York, NY

First originally published by Page Publishing, Inc. 2016

ISBN 978-1-68289-024-0

Printed in the United States of America

PREFACE

I was born November 8, 1966, to the late Pastor Webster Benjamin Turner and the late Mrs. Allie Mae Cooper Turner. I am the youngest of (dead and alive) eleven children born between the two.

I am a graduate of the former Wrens High School, Red River Area Vocational Technical School in Duncan, Oklahoma, of Phillips Junior College, and finally, of Augusta Technical College both in Augusta, Georgia. I am trained in building maintenance (plumbing, carpentry, and electrical studies). I have four years of naval science and ROTC training as top-ranking female overall and throughout the program. I achieve what I set out to accomplish.

My hobbies include preaching and teaching the Good News of God's kingdom, poetry, creative writing, art, singing, and working with computers. I am funny, loving, caring, and devoted. I strive to obey God and his son, Jesus Christ, rather than man. I reward and take pleasure in doing what is good while discovering what is bad or wrong. I do not support women's liberation since it does not agree with the teachings of the Bible. Submission, according to God's arrangement, is what I try to practice.

I have a loving and devoted husband. We are both dedicated and ordained ministers of Jehovah God. We have a spiritual family of more than 7 million others who believe and worship the way we do. Our hope is to live on the earth after God's victory over evil and Satan's final claim against Jehovah's right to rule over mankind. Then, we will live forever on the earth in a paradise.

I am a former quality assurance and treatment nurse, and a consultant student of the word of God. I am Hattie Denise Turner-Lewis, and this is my book. In it you will read about true-to-life events, situations, and memories of my life. I hope you will enjoy what you are about to read and experience. Finally, my writings include the beginning of my battle with bipolar manic-depressive disorder and severe depression. So I say to all, "Life doesn't end with what Satan puts upon us."

I'M NOT THE SAME

I used to drink till I passed out
Smoked cigarettes too without a doubt
I use to dance from dusk till dawn
I'm not the same 'cause I've been drawn.

Married men I used to date
To them I was known as jailbait
From my early teens I have been grown
I'm not the same, those days are gone.

Now I live for Jehovah God
I spread the news 'cause times are hard
My lifestyle now is true and divine
I'm not the same; God is the vine.

With all the things that I've been through,
I hope no one takes that course to pursue;
God is there to lean upon;
I'm not the same, I'm passing on.

So when this world comes to its end
Many I've known will not defend,
But all those on Jehovah's side
Who aren't the same, will win the prize.

I'M NOT FREE

Though I go as I please,
Have all the things I need,
I'm in bondage and cannot flee—
Here on earth I'm still not free.

At times I'm happy,
Sometimes miss my pappy
I'm a slave—yes that's me—
I am not safe and am not free.

White, red, yellow, and black—
These faces are all under attack
No need to fear your enemies;
Fear of them won't make you free.

Guilt-free I am
Not running a scam
A nonfree world is what I see.
One day soon, but now I'm not free.

HOW LONG?

God has no beginning that we know of,
He merely created us out of love.
From the dirt we were shaped and formed,
In the belly we were kept warm.

First came Heaven, then the earth
Animals then humans, Eve gave birth;
All creations were for God's Son
The plan from the start, we live as one.

Many have been sent to set things straight
No matter how many, their attempts were great
Since the final test is yet to come,
Be wise, my brothers, we're not done.

Since time began till now and so on,
God has been with us all along,
Precious gems formed out of the dust—
That's how Jehovah feels about us.

ARE YOU READY?

No need for tomorrow's birth
It's another day on God's green earth.
No time to spend with idle chat
It's just a game of this and that.

In time we'll learn our destiny
Prepare yourselves; this advice is free.
Determination motivates in time,
It's better we learn this in our prime.

There is a place that we all do go;
Most people are confused and do not know.

Peer knowledge states it is not true—
The dirt we walk on also made you.

Do you know what tomorrow brings?
If so, tell us about these things.
Now that you've heard, continue to study
So you can answer, "Are you ready?"

CLOSE

Though far away in time
It's coming 'cause it's divine
No hustle here, no game of luck;
It's soon to come, so pass the buck.

Before there was world to live,
Jehovah had plans, pure life to give
So here we are for a little while
Divine intervention will make you smile.

The closer we get, the further away
Our patience is needed if we should stay.
Pay close attention to the times—
The end is close, so don't be blind.

It's close at hand, our ears do hear
Above the law we should not steer
Obey Jehovah and wait on him
His light will brighten that which is dim.

TAKE A STAND

Don't be afraid to let it show
Speak out, be heard, let someone know,
Silence can harm when kept inside
So take a stand on Jehovah's side.

Don't give Satan a fighting chance
He'll lead you into an evil trance
Be firm, steadfast, and unmovable
The pressure is on, so be careful.

Life is a bowl of cherries—
Not true, there are no farriers
Lift up the divine name of Jehovah
Speak up, take a stand, don't roll over.

For years, men have always fought—
Fought for their country and the sort
Holy wars have claimed many
But to stand for Jah you gain plenty.

JEHOVAH AVENGES HIS PEOPLE

You did my soul a disfavor
Your superiors tried to savor
You both were wrong and out of line
I told you Jehovah was truly divine.

Choose your poison: pressure, death, or suffering
When messing with God the choice is unbearing
There is a thin line between love and hate
Fear for your life as it were; rejuvenate.

Mind how you talk to people so
For one day you may need to know
Live for the one who loved you first,
Don't mess with him or you may burst.

Jehovah avenges his people so true
Beware how you treat or avenged may be you
Safety comes only from God up above
Hold high his people and show much love.

MY DADDY

I never knew you but I've come to know
You were a very good man—your life showed.
One day I hope to see you in your entire array
I've dreamed of the moment, that very special day.
I was only an infant when you died long ago
I hope you'll be happy at the way I learned to go
I've missed all these years and I still do
I only hope I didn't somehow disappoint you
I have your picture on my mantelpiece;
The memory of you will never cease.
I have a picture of all of us too
From the oldest sibling down, we all resemble you
As I look at my baby picture on the stand
I see a bond between us only we understand.

THE LAST TIME

No more will I allow this pain
To cause me to suffer cloud and rain
I've taken all that I can bearNow to Jehovah I go to in prayer.

The hint has finally been seen
So as a fool, no more power is my dream
No more fighting, words, nor fists
Only the word of God and incense mists.

No more crying if you leave
Just move on ahead and also achieve
I love you dearly, this is true
But Jehovah gave me life, not you.

This is it, the very last time
You can do whatever, at the drop of a dime
I've talked to Jehovah—yes I've prayed
I've made him promise it will be obeyed.

FAMILY

Fathers and mothers are the start of it all
Brothers and sisters answer the family all
Children are a blessing from God;
Those who raise them should use the rod.
Uncles and aunts are special to know
Nephews and nieces born spoiled then go
Cousins and friends are distant and away
We keep in touch in a special way
Family life is like none I've ever seen
Through thick and thin, it smiles and gleams.
When I look at my extended family tree,
I can't help but wonder if they see what I see.
The family is the oldest institute
To have and to hold, there's no substitute.

BABYLON'S FALL
AND YOU

Babylon has fallen
And will fall again
But this time the fall
Will be worse than back then.

Poor Babylon, pretty as can be
All dolled up for a big catastrophe
Yes, she will be missed for some days
But soon her memory fades away.

So Christians don't be caught up with her
Nor even her company, do not bestir;
Her death-dealing ways are dangerous
So don't be caught under her monopolies.

The time is near, quite close you see
From "Babylon the Great" we all must flee
So stay close to Jehovah and his arrangement
Then we'll realize the prize for a life well spent.

FORGIVE THEM

For those who cast stones
For dogs that like bones
There's a reason for the teasing
Little minds, they need easing.

We have friends who hide their hands
Also dogs who wander on strange land

Teasing is their game of time
Something to do and mess with the mind.

Everyone has a little space
To occupy, I secure each place
Some invade; others turf too
To hurt, to harm, or just to pursue.

So Jehovah, I pray for all these ones
Whether scary with words or loaded guns
We are all children from one stem
So for their wrong, forgive them!

COMMITMENT

For the first time in my life
I recognize it's not a knife
I see this time it's not like church
It's straight ahead and requires research.

The introduction shook me up,
I expected wine from a dirty cup
It's not all that I thought it would be
I'm glad I took time to look and see.

Miraculous things were not promised at all
But through prayers and supplications it's just a mere call.
Be faithful and strong, give God his due;
You'll have no problems getting what's coming to you.

At death life begins on paradise earth
Where there is peace like a new birth.
My goal is to be there to see my loved ones
Then I'll be happy forever at home.

MOTHER

She protected me for nine whole months
When I was hid from eyes and felt no bumps
She fed me things I needed to have
She healed my wounds with healing.

No harm did she let come near to me
Thru storms and nights, she sat unselfishly
Well-to-do kisses with tickle and such
My mom showed she loved me very much.

Too young to leave alone, so Mom took me along
Her motto was "No children," well then, so long
She woke every time I moved the wrong way
I was sickly and required much care day after day

I had a good mother as all could see,
I didn't use to think so like it was to be
Seeing eye to eye was not practiced well
In most households, reasoning lacks a spell.

So I'm thankful I had a mother—
Something I could say like most others
Granted be strength to continue on in years
She brought me in the world with pain and tears.

BIPOLAR THE MIND

My mother was like a big sister then how
We talked on the phone and jawboned, powwow!
Like sisters we had our spats and quarrels
But love bound us both; we had good morals.

My mother was dear, sweet, and strong
No matter what, we got along.
You are to me a precious gem—great worth
I was very blessed to have had her who gave me birth

I'VE BEEN HERE WITH YOU ALL THE TIME

In the morning when you would rise
My dreams ended and for you compromised
Of all the times you thought you were alone
I've been here with you all along.

Though times are hard and seem not to end,
To Jehovah and Jesus, let every knee bend
Stronger bonds are like a sweet song
I've been here with you all along.

Pleasure seekers don't know why;
In fact, their type don't even try.
I'm glad your life has been prolonged;
I've been here with you all along.

Spiritual goodness shall follow you
All your life—yes, this is true
So I'll sing it out very strong,
"I've been here with you all along."

GRACIOUS, MERCIFUL, AND KIND

Gracious, merciful, and kind
Describes the Holy Divine
No greater friends could one have
Than Jehovah and his son, the Lamb.

Gracious, merciful, and kind
Shows that we're special in God's mind
As long as we believe and obey God,
We needn't worry 'bout the master's rod.

Gracious, merciful, and kind
Much comfort and peace in God we find.

We have a shelter in the time of the storm,
When we're naked and cold he keeps us warm.

Gracious, merciful, and kind
Describes God perfect as divine
Whatever we need or think we want,
Jehovah delivers when others don't.

LISTEN

When Jehovah speaks from the printed page
Apply to yourself in this present age
Hear him now while he may be heard
Listen intently to his every word

If you have ears then lend them close,
Beware of not hearing the soothing dose
Paying attention to mainly yourself;
Listen and change, don't put it on a shelf.

If your toes have been stepped on,
Work on it until the bad is gone
On your mark, get ready, set go,
Listen closely so you'll always know.

Expressions of love are spoken by God;
His son thus teaches with the rod.
Hearing the word is beneficial and true.
Listen, listen, and good always do.

MY LETTER TO JEHOVAH

Dear Jehovah, the one and only, who is most high
I am writing you for help, so hear my cry
First and foremost, Jehovah, help me to be a better person
With my present self I'm not satisfied, so help before it worsens.

Next I'd like to be a better wife, one who will submit
At present I rebel, resist, and make it hard for my crown to fit.
My tongue does not always build up, yet love my heart does crave
So help me, Father, before it's too late, before I reach my grave.

I'm mean as a snake, they say, I know this to be true
No need to hide the fact, I have the tendency to hate too
Along these lines let's work on this straight up and strong
With your help, dear Lord, I know we can't go wrong.

As I conclude I'd like to ask that you search me thru and thru
All that you find that doesn't fit get rid of it, let my heart be true.
Last but not least, just one more thing—I promise it is small
Set the alarm so when it's time, it'll wake us one and all.

Amen.

I HAVEN'T GIVEN UP

There used to be a place I'd go
To join my friends, to worship as you know
I'd hear the prayers and sing the songs
But most I learned right from wrong.

The Christian way was what I knew—
No doubts, no regrets, I gave God his due.
It used to be a career for me too:
To share the good news and Bible truths.

Although my career has been cut short
Jehovah still knows my Christian heart
I find it hard to pray sometimes
It's just Satan trying to blow my mind.

One day I'll go back to that little place
I'll see my friends and their loving face
I'll hear the prayer and sing the song
Most of all I'll prove Satan wrong.

The Christian way I'll resume again
No doubts, no regrets, but forgiven of sin
Although my career can no longer be
I still share the good news with all I see.

BIPOLAR THE MIND

Jehovah is the reason that I'm still here
Through nights of fear and many in tears
I'll continue to make the effort to pray and be heard
In hopes of eternal life, as promised in God's word.

THE PURE LANGUAGE

There is a language spoken today
A small group of people know what to say;
It's not in tongues of the unknown,
Proof of this language is widely shown.

Beware of false prophets here in the land
They speak with false words and always demand.
Proof of their falsehood is shown in their speech
For the true, pure language, they know not how to teach.

Come and join this small little band
Who speak the pure language in all the land.
Nobody knows it quite like they do
The true pure language they extend to you.

If you want to learn the language of love,
Listen to those I have listed up above.
There's no excuse not to know how to speak,
But to talk is easy when pure language you seek.

SATISFIED

I wish I were, but since I'm not,
I settle for this precious spot.
My way of life I use to hate
But now I'm free, as Satan's mate.
To say the least, I'm satisfied
For on the stake my Savior died.
To each his own, but we all know
Jehovah shows the way to go.
Life is short in this lifetime;
Let's make the best while in our prime.
In the final hour, on that last day,
Trust in Jehovah to show the way.

SAVIOR

S—one in which salvation may be found
A—the Almighty's only son
V—who has proven victorious over death
I—Instituted the covenant with the eleven disciples
O—Origin not of this world
R—mankind's Redeemer.

JESUS

J—Jehovah's only begotten son
E—an Effective preacher and teacher
S—Savior of mankind
U—exhibited unconditional love for mankind
S—will save all those loving Jehovah's Law.

FEED MY SHEEP

"If you love me," this he said,
"Continue my work 'cause I'm not dead."
The time will come to be cut short,
More time to preach, all times to sort.

"Feed my sheep," is what he said,
Understand the disciples were truly fed.
When Jesus ascended Heaven-bound,
His disciples were commissioned to herald the sound.

BELIEVE IN ME

Believe in me, I know the way
I work very hard to earn my pay
Monetary wages I do not take
Only Bible food, *The Watch Tower* and *Awake*.

Believe in me, I kid you not
The words I speak are spirit begot.
Jehovah is in Heaven—that is his home;
He gave the earth to man for him to roam.

Believe in me and do take notes,
Jehovah's word requires no votes.
Listen closely to what I say,
It may be helpful another day.

Believe in me, I finally say
Do all you can, Jehovah's way
Be strict, be bold, but mainly be strong;
Believe in me and prove Satan wrong.

IN GOD'S HOUSE

There is a place in all the lands
Where people go and take their stand
No matter who you bring, be it a friend or spouse,
All are welcome here in God's house.

A loving God is whom we serve,
A mighty force he's taught and learned.
Just carry the load apportioned to you,
In God's house, your duties are due.

Love fills this heavenly place of GodSafety
too can be found among the rods.
Be a part of this, it becomes you well,
Don't die without knowing the truth about Hell.

I'm just a drop in a bucket, so are you,
No one on earth is any better to do
Life is so wonderful, but that's not all
In God's house, life is eternal, in the parasitic call.

GOD'S WORD

When speaking about the Word of God,
Be gentle but firm; don't spare the rod.
A life of happiness can be had
But you make your own bed, good or bad.

Make yourself known as being smart—
Know when to speak, know how to start
Bubbling on in fooling speech
Wise up, read the Book and be complete.

Mumbo, jumbo, this, then that,
The Word of God just states the facts
Prayer and sincerity added to it
Make reading a good habit.

When times are hard and in a mess,
Reach for God's Word, learn from the best
At this late date, near to the end,
Don't be lost, on God depend.

HOME

Heaven is where God lives, the earth he gave to man
He put us here to cultivate and take care of the land
Although our lives may seem short here
Where eternity is spent, we need not fear.
We never think of why we die.
It all started in Eden, with Satan's lie
Now we are imperfect, with a price to pay
Death is the wage for sin; it is the only way.
We die for our sins to pay our dues
Then back to life to fulfill the Holy Bible truths.
Heaven is God's home; it is where he resides
He gave the earth to man; be content and satisfied.

A SINNER'S PRAYER

As I lay down my head to sleep
The Almighty knows my most inner deep
While I toss and turn through the night
I pray tomorrow I'll be all right
It seems as if the nights are long
Without my God I wouldn't be strong.
Now it's day and I give thanks again
So I beg the Master forgiveness of sin
Now night falls once upon another day
So I lay my head down and again I pray,
If I wake tomorrow morning, it is fine,
If not, God's will for me is divine.

PRAISES TO JEHOVAH

In the morning, in the noon
Never too early, never too soon
In the evening, late at night
Never too hasty, always polite.

Time of day matters not
Praises to Jehovah must be our lot,
Be on guard at all times;
We needn't worry in our prime.

Praises to Jehovah is a must
To ignore this privilege is like dust.
From time to time indefinite,
Praises to Jehovah should be permanent.

It's a joy to praise the Almighty
His works are not to be taken lightly.
Emotions and devotions are good to posses
Always remember, praise Jehovah and do not test.

JEHOVAH

J—The Divide Jude of both right and wrong
E—Defeats evolution theory all day long
H—Is for Heaven where Jehovah lives
O—He's King overall and generously gives
V—We are victims of Satan to be relieved soon
A—Avenger of human sufferings clear up to the moon
H—Those hungering for righteousness can and shall be fed
Jehovah has the power, even to raise up the dead.

MOTHER

She protected me for nine whole months
When I was hid from eyes and felt no bumps
She fed me things I needed to have
She healed my wounds with healing

No harm did she let come near to me
Thru storms and nights she sat unselfishly
Well-to-do kisses with tickle and such
My Mom showed she loved me very much

Too young to leave alone, so Mom took me along
Her motto was no children, well then so long
She woke every time I moved the wrong way
I was sickly and required much care day after day

I had a good Mother as all could see
I didn't use to think so like it was to be
Seeing eye to eye was not practiced well
In most households reasoning lacks a spell

So I'm thankful I had a Mother
Something I could say like most others
Granted be strength to continue on in years
She brought me in the world with pain and tears

BIPOLAR THE MIND

My Mother was like a big sister then how
We talked on the phone and jawboned powwow!
Like sisters we had our spats and quarrels
But LOVE binded us both, we had good morals

My Mother was dear, sweet, and strong
No matter what we got along
You are to me a precious GEM great worth
I was very blessed to have had, who gave me birth

MY DADDY

I never knew you but I've come to know
You were a very good man, your life showed
One day I hope to see you in your entire array
I've dreamed of the moment that very special day
I was only an infant when you died long ago
I hope you'll be happy at the way I learned to go
I've missed all these years and I still do
I only hope I didn't somehow disappoint you
I have your picture on my mantelpiece
The memory of you will never cease
I have a picture of all of us too
From the oldest sibling down, we all resemble you
As I look at my baby picture on the stand
I see a bond between us only we understand

THE LAST TIME

No more will I allow this pain
To cause me to suffer cloud and rain
I've taken all that I can bare
Now to Jehovah I go to in prayer

The hint has finally been seen
So as a fool, no more power is my dream
No more fighting, words, nor fists
Only the word of God and incense mists

No more crying if you leave
Just move on ahead and also achieve
I love you dearly this is true
But Jehovah gave me life, not you

This is it, the very last time
You can do whatever, at the drop of a dime
I've talked to Jehovah, yes I've prayed
I've made him promise it will be obeyed

FAMILY

Fathers and Mothers are the start of it all
Brothers and sisters answer the family call
Children are a blessing from God
Those who raise them should use the rod
Uncles and aunts are special to know
Nephews and nieces born spoiled then go
Cousins and friends are distant and away
We keep in touch in a special way
Family life is like none I've ever seen
Through thick and thin it smiles and gleams
When I look at my extended family tree
I can't help but wonder if they see what I see
The family is the oldest institute
To have and to hold, there's no substitute

BABYLONS FALL
AND YOU

Babylon has fallen
And will fall again
But this time the fall
Will be worse than back then

Poor Babylon, pretty as can be
All dolled up for a big catastrophe
Yes she will be missed for some days
But soon her memory fades away

So Christians don't be caught up with her
Nor even her company, do not bestir
Her death dealing ways are dangerous
So don't be caught under her monopolous

The time is near, quite close you see
From Babylon the Great we all must flee
So stay close to Jehovah and his arrangement
Then we'll realize the prize for a life well spent

FORGIVE THEM

For those who cast stones
For dogs that like bones
There's a reason for the teasing
Little minds they need easing

We have friends who hide their hands
Also dogs who wander on strange land

Teasing is their game of time
Something to do and mess with the mind

Everyone has a little space
To occupy I secure each place
Some invade others turf too
To hurt, to harm, or just to pursue

So Jehovah I pray for all these ones
Whether scary with words or loaded guns
We are all children from one stem
So for their wrong FORGIVE THEM!

COMMITMENT

For the first time in my life
I recognize it's not a knife
I see this time it's not like church
It's straight ahead and requires research

The introduction shook me up
I expected wine from a dirty cup
It's not all that I thought it would be
I'm glad I took time to look and see

Miraculous things were not promised at all
But through prayers and supplications it's just a mere call
Be faithful and strong, give God his due
You'll have no problems getting what's coming to you

At death life begins on paradise earth
Where there is peace like a new birth
My goal is to be there to see my loved ones
Then I'll be happy forever at home.

I'M NOT THE SAME

I use to drink till I passed out
Smoked cigarettes too without a doubt
I use to dance from dusk till dawn
I'm not the same cause I've been drawn

Married men I use to date
To them I was known as jail-bait
From my early teens I have been grown
I'm not the same, those days are gone

Now I live for Jehovah God
I spread the news cause times are hard
My lifestyle now is true and divine
I'm not the same, God is the vine

With all the things that I've been through
I hope no one takes that course to pursue
God is there to lean upon
I'm not the same, I'm passing on

So when this world comes to its end
Many I've known will not defend
But all those on Jehovah's side
Who aren't the same, will win the prize

I'M NOT FREE

Though I go as I please
Have all the things I need
I'm in bondage and Cannot flee
Here on earth I'm still not free

At times I'm happy
Sometimes miss my pappy
I'm a slave, yes that's me
I am not safe and am not free

White, red, yellow, and black
These faces are all under attack
No need to fear your enemies
Fear of them won't make you free

Guilt-free I am
Not running a scam
A non-free world is what I see
One day soon but now I'm not free

HOW LONG?

God has no beginning that we know of
He merely created us out of love
From the dirt we were shaped formed
In the belly we were kept warm

First came Heaven, then the earth
Animals then humans, Eve gave birth
All creations were for God's son
The plan from the start, we live as one

Many have been sent to set things straight
No matter how many their attempts were great
Since the final test is yet to come
Be wise my brothers we're not done

Since time began till now and so on
God has been with us all long
Precious gems formed out of the dust
That's how Jehovah feels about us

MY LETTER TO JEHOVAH

Dear Jehovah, the one and only, who is most high
I am writing you for help, so hear my cry
First and foremost, Jehovah, help me to be a better person
With my present self I'm not satisfied, so help before it worsens

Next I'd like to be a better wife, one who will submit
At present I rebel, resist, and make it hard for my crown to fit
My tongue does not always build up yet love my heart does crave
So help me Father before its too late, before I reach my grave

I'm mean as a snake they say, I know this to be true
No need to hide the fact, I have the tendency to hate too
Along these lines let's work on this straight up and strong
With your help Dear Lord I know we can't go wrong

As I conclude I'd like to ask that you search me thru and thru
All that you find that doesn't fit get rid of it, let my heart be true
Last but not least, just one more thing, I promise it is small
Set the alarm so when it's time it'll wake us one and all

AMEN

I HAVEN'T GIVEN UP

There use to be a place I'd go
To join my friends, to worship as you know
I'd hear the prayers and sing the songs
But most I learned right from wrong

The Christian way was what I knew
No doubts, no regrets, I gave God his due
It use to be a career for me too
To share the good news and Bible truths

Although my career has been cut short
Jehovah still knows my Christian heart
I find it hard to pray sometimes
It's just Satan trying to blow my mind

One day I'll go back to that little place
I'll see my friends and their loving face
I'll hear the prayer and sing the song
Most of all I'll prove Satan wrong

The Christian way I'll resume again
No doubts, no regrets, but forgiven of sin
Although my career can no longer be
I still share the good news with all I see

BIPOLAR THE MIND

Jehovah is the reason that I'm still here
Through nights of fear and many in tears
I'll continue to make the effort to pray and be heard
In hopes of eternal life as promised in God's word

THE PURE LANGUAGE

There is a language spoken today
A small group of people know what to say
It's not in tongues of the unknown
Proof of this language is widely shown

Beware of false prophets here in the land
They speak with false words and always demand
Proof of their falsehood is shown in their speech
For the true pure language they know not how to teach

Come and join this small little band
Who speak the pure language in all the land
Nobody knows it quite like they do
The true pure language they extend to you

If you want to learn the language of love
Listen to those I have listed up above
There's no excuse not to know how to speak
But to talk is easy when pure language you seek

SAVIOR

S- one in which salvation may be found
A- the almighty's only son
V- who has proven Victorious over death
I- Instituted the covenant with the 11 disciples
O- Origin not of this world
R- mankind's Redeemer

JESUS

J- Jehovah's only begotten son
E- an Effective preacher and teacher
S- Savior of mankind
U- exhibited Unconditional love for mankind
S- will Save all those loving Jehovah's Law

FEED MY SHEEP

If you love me, this he said
Continue my work cause I'm not dead
The time will come to be cut short
More time to preach all times to sort

Feed my sheep, is what he said
Understand the disciples were truly fed
When Jesus ascended Heaven-bound
His disciples were commissioned to herald the sound

BELIEVE IN ME

Believe in me, I know the way
I work very hard to earn my pay
Monetary wages I do not take
Only Bible food, The Watchtower and Awake

Believe in me, I kid you not
The words I speak are spirit begot
Jehovah is in Heaven, that is his home
He gave the earth to man, for him to roam

Believe in me and do take notes
Jehovah's word requires no votes
Listen closely to what I say
It may be helpful another day

Believe in me, I finally say
Do all you can, Jehovah's way
Be strict, be bold, but mainly be strong
Believe in me and prove Satan wrong

IN GOD'S HOUSE

There is a place in all the lands
Where people go and take their stand
No matter who you bring, be a friend or spouse
All are welcome, here in God's house

A loving God is whom we serve
A mighty force he's taught and learned
Just carry the load apportioned to you
In God's house your duties are due

Love fills this heavenly place of God's
Safety too can be found among the rods
Be a part of this, it becomes you well
Don't die without knowing the truth about hell

I'm just a drop in a bucket, so are you
No one on earth is any better to do
Life is so wonderful, but that's not all
In god's house, life is eternal, in the parasitic call

GOD'S WORD

When speaking about the Word of God
Be gentle, but firm, don't spare the rod
A life of happiness can be had
But you make your own bed, good or bad

Make yourself Known, as being smart
Know when to speak, know how to start
Bubbling on in fooling speech
Wise up, read "The Book", be complete

Mumbo, Jumbo, this, then that
The Word of God just states the facts
Prayer and sincerity added to it
Make reading a good habit

When times are hard and in a mess
Reach for God's Word, learn from the best
At this lat date, near to the end
Don't be lost, on God depend

HOME

Heaven is where God lives, the earth he gave to man
He put us here to cultivate and take care of the land
Although our lives may seem short here
Where eternity is spent, we need not fear
We never think of why we die
It all started in Eden, with Satan's lie
Now we are imperfect, with a price to pay
Death is the wage for sin, it is the only way
We die for our sins to pay our dues
Then back to life to fulfill the Holy Bible truths
Heaven is God's home; it is where he resides
He gave the earth to man, be content and satisfied

A SINNER'S PRAYER

As I lay down my head to sleep
The Almighty knows my most inner deep
While I toss and turn through the night
I pray tomorrow I'll be all right
It seems as if the nights are long
Without my God I wouldn't be strong
Now it's day and I give thanks again
So I beg the Master forgiveness of sin
Now night falls once upon another day
So I lay my head down and again I pray
If I wake tomorrow morning, it is fine
If not, God's will for me is divine

PRAISES TO JEHOVAH

In the morning, in the noon
Never too early, never too soon
In the evening, late at night
Never too hasty, always polite

Time of day matters not
Praises to Jehovah must be our lot
Be on guard at all times
We needn't worry in our prime

Praises to Jehovah is a must
To ignore this priviledge is like dust
From time to time indefinite
Praises to Jehovah should be permanent

It's a joy to praise the almighty
His works are not to be taken lightly
Emotions and devotions are good to posses
Always remember, praise Jehovah and do not test

JEHOVAH

J- The Divide Jude of both right and wrong
E- Defeats Evolution Theory all day long
H- Is for Heaven where Jehovah lives
O- He's King Over all and generously gives
V- we are Victims of Satan to be relieved soon
A- Avenger of human sufferings clear up to the moon
H- those hungering for righteousness can and shall be fed
JEHOVAH has the power, even to raise up the dead

ARE YOU READY?

No need for tomorrow's birth
It's another day on God's green earth
No time to spend with idle chat
It's just a game of this and that

In time we'll learn our destiny
Prepare yourselves this advice is free
Determination motivates in time
It's better we learn this in our prime

There is a place that we all do go
Most people are confused and do not know

Peer knowledge states it is not true
The dirt we walk on also made you

Do you know what tomorrow brings
If so tell us about these things
Now that you've heard continue to study
So you can answer, "ARE YOU READY?

CLOSE

Though far away in time
It's coming cause It's divine
No hustle here, no game of luck
It's soon to come so pass the buck

Before there was world to live
Jehovah had plans, pure life to give
So here we are for a little while
Divine intervention will make you smile

The closer we get the further away
Our patience is needed if we should stay
Pay close attention to the times
The end is close so don't be blind

It's close at hand, our ears do hear
Above the law we should not steer
Obey Jehovah and wait on him
His light will brighten that which is dim

TAKE A STAND

Don't be afraid to let it show
Speak out, be heard, let someone know
Silence can harm when kept inside
So take a stand on Jehovah's side

Don't give Satan a fighting chance
He'll lead you into an evil trance
Be firm, steadfast, and unmovable
The pressure is on so be careful

Life is a bowl of cherries
Not true, there are no farriers
Lift up the divine name of Jehovah
Speak up, take a stand, don't roll over

For years men have always fought
Fought for their country and the sort
Holy wars have claimed many
But to stand for Jah you gain plenty

JEHOVAH AVENGES HIS PEOPLE

You did my soul a disfavor
Your superiors tried to savor
You both were wrong and out of line
I told you Jehovah was truly divine

Choose your poison, pressure, death, or suffering
When messing with God the choice is unbearing
There is a thin line between love and hate
Fear for your life, as it were, rejuvenate

Mind how you talk to people so
For one day you may need to know
Live for the one who loved you first
Don't mess with him or you may burst

Jehovah avenges his people so true
Beware how you treat or avenged may be you
Safety comes only from God up above
Hold high his people and show much love

I'VE SHARED MY LIFE WITH YOU

There are no thoughts that you don't know
There are no places we cannot go
No doors are closed to you at all
No windows are shut that you can't uninstall.

My life is naked to you alone
Free as a bird in a tow-free zone
Secrets are nothing between us two
What God put together, man can't undo.

Building life means sharing time
You and I have spent many dimes
Been through it all together as one
Will continue on till all is done.

I shared my entire life with you,
No regrets or mistakes to render due
This life will be over soon, then we'll be
Together forever and ever eternally.

NO ONE KNEW

Behind closed doors it used to be
The outside world just could not see
The skeletons in the closets too
Were shameful things no one should do.

When the time came to give account
No one could say cause there was doubt
The secrets that come people keep
The scary thought from the inner deep.

Let no one say he knows it all
For fear that he may take a fall
It's hard to say what happened here
But for sure one fled out of fear.

No one knew and never said
All we know is he is dead.
Bless this family, especially now
Teach them to pray, for they don't know how.

A LOVE THAT IS FOR REAL

(FAMILY LOVE)

A love that gives is a love that lives
A love that dares is a love that shares
A love that that greets is a love that meets
A love that prays is a love that stays
A love that trusts is a love that must
A love that cries is an effort; it tries
A love that counts the cost
Need not fear being lost!

REMEMBER HOW WE USED TO BE

I've often thought your word was gold
You spoke, you said; what you meant was told.
Now you've changed and although you speak
The words you say are all unique
The promises you made a long time ago
Were just words you said to have your say, you know.
You've hurt me much, yes, every day it seems
This is because I love you most; you're my self-esteem
Although our lives have changed so much
Our hearts still seem to keep in touch
Can we just go back to the way we were?
We might discover that life then was sure.
I used to respect you and call you sir
Now I see you as just another coffee stir
Don't get me wrong, I still love you so
And you don't have to worry; I'll never let you go
But please, for our love's sake, think before you threat;
Remember, I'm the last real woman you'll ever meet.

FRIENDS

Everyone has them, it's plain to see
But are they true, faithful, and free
If push came to shove would they die for you
Or would they just hide like others do?

In time of need, can you count on them
Or do you find your needs a stranger called Jim
Do they egg you on in wrong deeds,
But when you're caught, who takes the lead?

Are you often along when times are hard
Then when you're with cash the party starts?
How can you tell who to trust with your hand
Who will be there thru it all, to help you stand?

To test true friendship, take the first step
Be all that you can and always go the depth
Follow Jehovah's and Jesus's example of showing love
Be at peace with yourself and trust in the friends above.

BLACK IS BEAUTIFUL

I'm black and proud, I love my race
Though there are some who hide their face
A man is a man no matter the color of their skin
But in this world, if you're black, you must defend.
Since way back when and it's always been
We've fought against ourselves for the white men
My beautiful black people don't sell out
We are in high places, so spread some clout
Once we make it to the top, always remember,
The ones we pass going up should be treated tender
The beauty of blackness is shown worldwide
Black men have business; black women have their pride
It's a pleasure and privilege to be known as black;
We've come a long way, now, from those plantation shacks.

AS I LIVE AND BREATHE

Through it all, I have become
The one to lean on for anyone
What got me to this point and place
Was carrying a smile upon my face.

As I live and breathe,
I go down on my knees
I pray for strength to bear
Not just mine but also others' burdens to share.

My past, I am not very proud of;
Many heartaches and much lack of love
Remorse, regrets, and downright hopelessness
All give evidence of being powerless.

As I live and breathe,
I go down on my knees
I pray for guidance to follow
The right direction for tomorrow.

YOU

There are no better words to say
Than to make somebody's day
These words I say of you are true
Much love and trust I found in you
No greater joy than one can find
A friendship that is true and kind
Jehovah sent you straight to me
So, friend of mine, let our friendship run free.

THOSE ARE THE
DAYS OF OUR LIVES

Although we have our falling outs
We love each other without a doubt
In spite of all that we've been thru,
Ten years isn't enough to call it true.

You're the light of my life; I love you so,
So whenever you get mad, don't up and go
Reveal your thoughts, but don't provoke
Our relationship is special, not a joke.

Be mindful of the things you say
They may come back and haunt one day
Tic-tac-toe and tit-for-tat are games
But what we live needs not be lame.

For the final word on lecturing you,
I can't omit my back rubs past due
So as you crawl into bed tonight,
Instead of the pillow, squeeze me tight.

MY SISTER

S—You're the sister I've always dreamed about
I—In times of trouble you're always there without a doubt
S—You're someone I have come to love more
T—Together we can open many doors
E—Eternal life, has been promised by God
R—Remember me even when times are hard.

LOVE

L is for longevity is marriage of course
O is obligation to the one you love
V is for venting and showing remorse
E is for eternal and divine from above.

GET WELL SOON

Just a few words to say to you
In hopes that they may comfort too,
Rest assured that when I pray,
Your name is mentioned in a special way.
I love you sis, with all my heart
Although we are hundreds of miles apart.
So, get well soon and don't delay
A wish for a speedy recovery is on the way.

THE INEVITABLE

I used to fear it most of all
The thought, the feel, its backing call
I've seen it time and time again
The very sight crawls up my skin
I know one day, it's gonna come
Though how or when, it's not like some.
At times I've wanted to end this jail
Three times or more, I've tried and failed
Family and friends seem not to care,
But it's me who loves me enough to bear
Soon it'll be over and I will be free
The fear of dying will not bother me.

MY SPECIAL DAY

Nothing would please me more than this
For someone to send me on a heavenly bliss
I'd love even more a day set aside
To show hospitality to me with great pride.
It's nice to tell me I'm special, you see,
But it's just not the same as a special day would be
Give me my flowers while I am alive
Because once I'm dead my nose is deprived
Just for a moment; an hour or two to spare,
Make me feel special, what a moment to share
My special day, I wonder how will it be
All dressed up and pretty for the world to see.
Family will be there to make the day great
Remember, it's my special day, so don't be late.

LOVE'S RAINBOW

Red, yellow, white, and blue
The color of love is seen in you
There is a certain way you know
The things you do, that love you show.
Black, orange, purple, and green
The color of love is sometimes mean
To fuss and fight may starve a life
The smallest word cuts like a knife.
Love's rainbow is colorful indeed
It takes all colors to fulfill love's need
Rainbows are pretty, colorful, and bright
Love rainbows are precious in darkness and in light.

A LOVE THAT IS FOR REAL

(FAMILY LOVE)

A love that gives, is a love that lives
A love that dares, is a love that shares
A love that that greets, is a love that meets
A love that prays, is a love that stays
A love that trusts, is a love that must
A love that cries, is an effort, it tries
A love that counts the cost
Need not fear being lost!

LOVE AND FORGIVENESS

If you truly love and it is to give
Hurtful things you will forgive
Love and forgiveness go hand in hand,
Both are from God, so don't demand.

A loved one can feel a truthfulness;
Love and forgiveness is shown to confess.
"Be wise, my son," the good book states,
Don't worry about those little mistakes.

Love and forgiveness is to be shared
Divided evenly, life is spared
No need to fear the things unknown,
Love and forgiveness give life to the bones.

Surely you know just what to do—
If feelings are hurt, give them their due
Expect the best and goodwill come
Have love and forgiveness, an equal sum.

THE BROTHERHOOD

I love my fleshly family—true,
But not the way I give the brotherhood their due
My fleshly family will be there sometimes
But the brotherhood is always on the receiving line.

The brotherhood is bound by God to love
Not just with their heart but also their blood
The brotherhood is expected to do so much
Treat brothers as men, the sisters with a delicate touch.

The family is the first institution by God;
It's the oldest and most precious yet governed by the rod
The brotherhood belongs to Jehovah as his slaves
But there is no such thing as shackles and caves

On Lord, one faith, one baptism, and one God
No over and out, no betweens, no down trods
These words I am speaking are all very true
It behooves you to listen and then apply them to you.

THIS IS MY LOVER'S PRAYER

A beauty queen I may not be,
God put my beauty inside of me
Fancy clothes I do not wear,
If clothes made me I wouldn't care.
I've often talked to God about us;
In God we must put all of our trust.
Let's guard our love as a matter of prayer
So we'll be sure and know, it'll always be there.

MY TOE

From the top of his head
To the bottom of his feet
The man is a man—my man
My toe is strong, yet so sweet.

He's respected by me and others too;
His household is cared for well.
No harm to his family will there be
My toe takes care of . . . they tell.
Life without him cannot be
No one could ever take his place;
Knowing he's with me, I'm at peace,
My toe has power; he puts a smile on my face

Me and our future children are number two
Of course we know Jehovah is first,
Then come our mothers who gave us life
My toe has a heart that's large enough to trust.

I UNDERSTAND NOW

For all the times that you were sad
Inside, you also felt quite mad
I remember the times that you were hurt,
The pain was deep, you felt like dirt.

No words can bring you back to us now
If there were a way I'd find out how
You suffered much in many ways,
Long were the nights and hard were the days.

I did not get to know you well
But the you I knew was kind of swell.
I miss the *Saturday Soul Train* line,
We never missed it; we were always on time.

Believe it or not, I grew up to see
Another battered wife like you used to be
The wife turned out to be me, of course
It finally ended in a silent divorce.

I started a new, which is better now
After ten whole years we should know how
We are both ordained ministers of God,
We know better; we control the rod.

HATTIE LEWIS

I miss you, big sister, after all these years
Twenty-six years and I'm still in tears
The way you died was peaceful in your sleep
But you could have lived longer if you'd thought very deep.

Now I've attempted suicide four or more times
For some reason why, God keeps saving my dimes
I have this illness that typifies death
But with all I've got, I should savor by breath.

Momma is old now and Grandma is dead
Uncle Solomon is sick and on his last leg
And you are a grandma of five or more
I say that because Tavie knocks on many doors.

I don't have any kids yet
But before I'm forty I'll have one, you bet
I think I'm ready for motherhood.
I remember your example—it was good.

I can't help but think you were so young,
Twenty years old—your life had just begun.
Our brother too, had his life cut short
I'll look for both at the Eternal Airport.

Now just recently we lost big sis
Although she's not suffering, she will be missed
She suffered a while, but not too long
God knew she was weak and not that strong.

To name you all, it hurts me so
I feel such sorrow and I can't let go
First, Daddy, then you now, Darnella too.
It's scary to think of the next number due.

I've enjoyed our little talk tonight

BIPOLAR THE MIND

Though one sided, I feel alright
In closing, I say, "I understand now
The sadness, the pain, yes, I know how."

I love you!

I'M NOT AFRAID ANYMORE

Go ahead, pack up, leave me alone;
I haven't time for game
I've learned to have a heart of stone
No more heartaches to claim.

You're not the only man alive
I'm not a mangy dog
I can have someone else with pride,
Or else live all alone.

I used to fear being alone at night
But no more; I fear the day.
Since leaving is your claim and flight,
Go ahead, try me, I won't make you stay.

Farewell, dear heart, go find yourself
I know who I am and want to be
Me, myself, and I may sit up on a shelf
But when the time is right, I'll know it's right for me.

I'm not afraid anymore
You can't make me quake.
So turn and walk right out the door;
Not one tear will I make.

BAD VIBES

I came to you for help
The type was needed bad
I came to you for comfort
For I was oh so sad,

You offered help and then some
Inappropriately, you were sick
My vulnerability was spotted
That's when you poured it on thick.

When I began to return it
You acted like you didn't know
You were wrong in your deception
But then came the fatal blow.

Operation saved a heart
Once bitten, twice shy.
Now I am healing up
So, stay away or else, die.

COMMON LINK

I need you; you're my better half
Sparks still flick in my heart
Together all these years and you still make me laugh.

Speak easy, soft, and slow
Though some people don't realize
But as true Christians we know.

Encourage the lowly one;
Share joy with the meek;
Follow the example of God's Son;
Simple facts are known to us,
It's hard at time without English
But what we know most is calculus.

Religious ties are common,
Politics—we take no part;
Faithful ones shall summon.

NO ONE ESCAPES ME

I hear what you are saying
I know the words oh so well,
The thoughts that you are thinking
Are not thoughts I cannot tell.

You try to be so smart and sharp
You lose touch with your mind;
No one can tell you anything
The word is full of selfish time.

I'm all over ones like you;
I've got you down is black and white.
You make my inside fold right out
I merely want to fuss and flight.

There's nothing you can say or do—
No moves, no games, no motives
I've been and seen most everything
So bring it on, so what gives

Now you've got me ticked off
I'm ready to burst or explode
Remember, no one escapes me
My life resolves such modes.

I'VE SHARED MY
LIFE WITH YOU

There are no thoughts that you don't know
There are no places we cannot go
No doors are closed to you at all
No windows are shut that you can't uninstall,

My life is naked to you alone
Free as a bird in a tow-free zone
Secrets are nothing between us two
What God put together man can't undo

Building life means sharing time
You and I have spent many dimes
Been through it all together as one
Will continue on till all is done

I shared my entire life with you
No regrets or mistakes to render due
This life will be over soon, then we'll be
Together forever and ever eternally.

SHARING

When you're in love with someone
There is no need to carry a ton,
Two people share responsibility;
Lighten the load to make it easy.

The saying goes and is often better,
"A family that prays, stays together."
Togetherness is good for family;
It soothes the souls and builds the tree.

Sharing is caring in all sorts of ways
It builds relations and in riches it pays
Love among friends is solid and true
Never underestimate the friendship's clue.

Always be willing to share a little;
Don't try to bare it from the middle
Beware of those who will weight you down
But continue to help those who share common ground.

I'M A DREAMER

At night as I close my eyes
My mind wake up to visualize
I see new things like never before
But really they're locked up in a memory door.

I'm a dreamer that dreams a lot;
Everyone dreams but some cannot.
My dreams take me far, far away
Sometimes I dream and wish I could stay.

I dream of being a movie star—
One driving around in a fancy car.
Of course it's only just a dream
So what, let me be a one-man team.

Some nights I don't dream at all—
I become afraid and begin to call;
My mind then wakes up to visualize
It remembers what to do when I close my eyes.

FIND ME

Today I'm this, tomorrow I'm that
This game I'm in is tit for tat
I wish I were like other were
I'd live my life like I prefer
My life is all scrambled up you see
I'm more than one, or two, or three
It is a shame to hold inside oneself
The pain, the grief—an empty shelf.
Just for a day I'd like to know how
It would feel to be normal right now
Maybe I'm crazy, mean, or even dumb
But I'm still a human and not some bum
So if you see me, don't turn away
See me as someone who needs help today!

GETTING OLD

Today is a day, just an ordinary day
The only difference is my life's new way
Some years ago, though no chance of my own
Someone up there, my future had known
All of these years, I've wondered why
I've lived so long and not yet died
I've experiences many things, some not understood
Of course thru the years no one really would
We are born, we are raised, and before we can know
The life that was given is like hot sun on snow
So today is a day, just an ordinary day
I won't take it for granted, for it's another new day.

REMARKS TO THE OTHER ME

In times of need you're always there
To comfort me in my worst despair
No one knows me quite like you
The smallest things I say or do.

I'm glad I got you for myself;
I couldn't be happy with no one else
Loving you comes so natural to me
It's like it was and always will be.

There is a certain way you are
Like on TV, my private movie star
I'll love you throughout eternity and more;
Jehovah will bless us, there's much in store
Sometimes I'm mean not quite all there
My promise to you, is I'll always care
The me I am now is the me you are
I love the other me like a priceless star.

Don't ever leave me; I couldn't adjust
I'd just curl up and die and hope for the best
Nobody knows the secrets we keep
It'll be buried with us in the hell so deep.

HATTIE LEWIS

I just can't imagine no other me
How lonely we'd be, but not fancy free
If I've ever hurt us, I'm sorry, you know,
Sometimes I forget how we need us so.

Since the day we met our other self
We put our trust in the other me for help
Screamin' demons have hated that day;
Joe Lewis, the other me, came my way.

I love you, Babe, so never forget
Dreams are for dreamers but true love is no bet
I'll always be with you, even after life's death
Don't worry, Babe, you'll always be mine till my very last breath.

NOT MY CHOICE

November 8th I did arrive,
Not my choice, but I'm alive
The last to come for he and she,
Together they made a little old one.

A bundle of joy with breath to sigh
Not my choice, but still I'd cry
On other sibling to call my own
Not knowing the future, but now she gone.

Others there are, but is there love
This answer can only come from above
I love my brothers and sisters too
Expected in return, I hope they do.

Not my choice, but I'm here
No one to blame but there is fear
He left me when I did not know
The difference between my head or toe.

If I'm a problem stay away
Don't pretend with me, that's not my way
Memories they have, but I'm not there
I hurt within cause, what pain I bear.

My success is due to her
She raised me up with ma'am and sirs
The life now makes a difference to me
I'm glad I stayed and she feels free.

A recognition I would like
Ashamed of me, then take a hike
Deep inside that means a lot
Protect me now, my choice it's not.

Words can cut you like knife
Silence ignores, but hey that's life
To be left out can really hurt
So take the hint know were dirt.

The one above has plans for me
Not my choice but hear my plea
Remember me now before I'm gone
Thou not my choice my life's a loan.

Not my choice, but I do care
A senseless gem is truth or dare
Love me not each one of you
Recognize me I'm from him too.

About the Author

Hattie's father was a minister and her mother was a strong minded woman, even though they had "a real God but not according to accurate knowledge" Romans 10:2. She thanks them dearly for raising her the way she is because they challenged her to ask questions such as "Why are we here? What the bible says, about what happened years and years ago? If there is one God, why do men worship him differently, after all we are all his creations?"

CPSIA information can be obtained at www.ICGtesting.com
Printed in the USA
BVOW08s2319260416

445689BV00001BA/29/P